BY VALERIE BODDEN

CREATIVE EDUCATION

Published by Creative Education
P.O. Box 227, Mankato, Minnesota 56002
Creative Education is an imprint of The Creative Company
www.thecreativecompany.us

Design and production by The Design Lab
Art direction by Rita Marshall
Printed by Corporate Graphics in the United States of America

Photographs by 123RF (Roman Krochuk), Corbis (Bjorn Backe/
Papilio, Images.com, NASA/Roger Ressmeyer, Stocktrek, Ron
Watts), Dreamstime (Romko), iStockphoto (David T. Gomez,
Hakan Karlsson, Roman Krochuk, Constance McGuire, John
Pitcher, Shawn Waite), Minneapolis Public Library, Minneapolis
Collection, NASA/ESA/John Clarke (University of Michigan),
National Oceanic and Atmosphere Administration (NOAA) Photo
Library/Historic NWS Collection, The Nobel Foundation

Library of Congress Cataloging-in-Publication Data
Bodden, Valerie.
Northern lights / by Valerie Bodden.
p. cm. — (Big outdoors)
Summary: A fundamental introduction to the northern lights,
including the atmosphere that makes them possible, the northern
creatures that live under them, and how people are affected by them.
Includes index.
ISBN 978-1-58341-818-5
1. Auroras—Juvenile literature. I. Title. II. Series.

QC971.4.B63 2010
538'.768—dc22   2009004691

CPSIA: 121510 PO1414
9 8 7 6 5 4 3

BIG OUTDOORS
NORTHERN LIGHTS

NORTH POLE

The northern lights are lights that can be seen in the sky at night. They appear in areas close to the North Pole. Most often, the northern lights shine above the state of Alaska and parts of the countries of Canada, Greenland, and Iceland.

Most people who can see the northern lights live in cold places

Some people think the northern lights make a "swishing" or "crackling" sound.

The northern lights shine all
the time. But they are easiest
to see during the fall, winter,
and spring, when the nights
are longest. The lights can
be many colors.
But green is
the most
common
color.

The northern lights are formed by **particles** that travel through space from the sun. Some of the particles hit Earth's **magnetic field**. They become filled with electricity. They are pulled toward the North Pole. There they run into **gases** in the **atmosphere** (*AT-mohs-feer*). That makes them glow different colors.

The sun is a big star that gives light and warmth to Earth

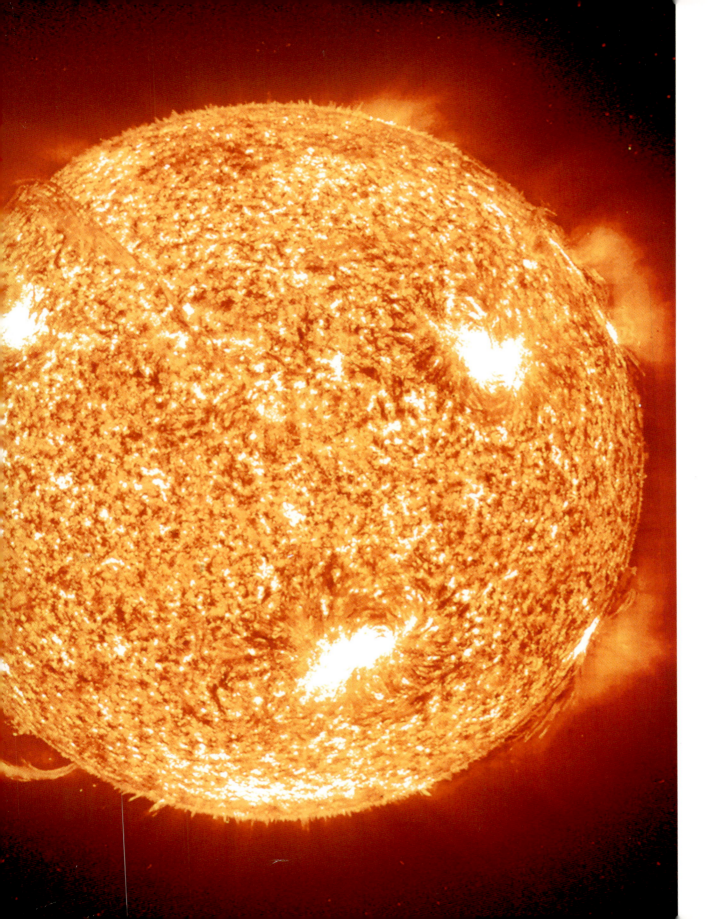

Sometimes the northern lights look like curtains, ribbons, or arches.

The weather in the areas where the northern lights shine is often cold. There are many small towns beneath the northern lights. But there are not many big cities.

Not many people live close to the brightest northern lights

In some places, the northern lights shine over forests. In other places, the ground is covered with short grasses or wildflowers. Some areas have only snow and ice.

The northern lights can be seen over snowy mountain forests

The sun blocks people's view of the northern lights during the day.

Animals that like cold weather live beneath the northern lights. Polar bears live in some areas. Moose and wolves live in other places.

Polar bears (opposite) and moose (above) have warm fur

People have told stories about the northern lights for thousands of years. Some stories say the northern lights are dancers. Today, scientists study the northern lights with **satellites**.

The northern lights can move and change shapes throughout the night.

Since the northern lights are high up in the atmosphere, people cannot affect them. But sometimes the northern lights affect life on Earth. Electric **currents** created by the northern lights can make people's power go out.

Electricity from power plants controls the lights in homes

Every year, many people travel to the far north to see the northern lights. They watch outside on dark, clear nights. They are amazed by the bright lights that swirl across the sky!

Some people drive a long way to watch the northern lights

There are "southern lights" that shine above the South Pole.

Lights like Earth's northern lights shine above planets such as Jupiter, too.

Glossary

atmosphere the layer of gases that surrounds Earth

currents flows of electricity; they are made up of particles that are all filled with electricity

gases airlike substances that have no shape

magnetic field an invisible area around a magnet in which the pull of the magnet can be felt; Earth acts like a giant magnet, so it has a magnetic field

particles tiny pieces of something

satellites machines that go around Earth in outer space

Read More about It

Dwyer, Mindy. *Northern Lights A to Z.* Seattle: Sasquatch Books, 2007.

Piehl, Janet. *Northern Lights.* Minneapolis: Lerner Publications, 2009.

Index